T0034851

# better together*

*This book is best read together, grownup and kid.

akidsco.com

a
kids
book
about

# a kids book about

# EQUALITY

## by Billie Jean King

**A Kids Co.**
**Editor** Jelani Memory
**Designer and Creative Director** Rick DeLucco
**Studio Manager** Konya Feldes
**Sales Director** Melanie Wilkins
**Head of Books** Jennifer Goldstein
**CEO and Founder** Jelani Memory

**DK**
**Editor** Emma Roberts
**Senior Production Editor** Jennifer Murray
**Senior Production Controller** Louise Minihane
**Senior Acquisitions Editor** Katy Flint
**Managing Art Editor** Vicky Short
**Publishing Director** Mark Searle

This American Edition, 2024
Published in the United States by DK Publishing
1745 Broadway, 20th Floor, New York, NY 10019

DK, a Division of Penguin Random House LLC

Text and design copyright © 2022 by Billie Jean King Enterprises, Inc.
A Kids Book About, Kids Are Ready, and the colophon 'a' are trademarks of A Kids Book About, Inc.
23 24 25 26 27  10 9 8 7 6 5 4 3 2 1
001-339149-Jan/2024

All rights reserved. Without limiting the rights under the copyright reserved above,
no part of this publication may be reproduced, stored in or introduced into a retrieval system,
or transmitted, in any form, or by any means (electronic, mechanical, photocopying, recording,
or otherwise), without the prior written permission of the copyright owner.
Published in Great Britain by Dorling Kindersley Limited.

A catalog record for this book is available from the Library of Congress.
ISBN: 978-0-7440-9463-3

DK books are available at special discounts when purchased in bulk for
sales promotions, premiums, fund-raising, or educational use. For details, contact:
DK Publishing Special Markets, 1745 Broadway, 20th Floor, New York, NY 10019, or SpecialSales@dk.com

Printed and bound in China

**www.dk.com**

**akidsco.com**

This book was made with Forest
Stewardship Council™ certified
paper – one small step in DK's
commitment to a sustainable future.
**For more information go to
www.dk.com/our-green-pledge**

For the children of the world:
be true to yourselves, and may you stay
strong and forever young at heart.

# Intro
## for grownups

When I was 12 years old, I was sitting at the Los Angeles Tennis Club thinking about my sport. I noticed everyone playing tennis around me wore white clothes and everyone playing was white. I asked myself, "Where is everyone else?" Even at that young age, I knew something wasn't right, and from that day forward, I committed myself to championing equality.

Inclusion lives at the heart of equality, and understanding inclusion largely comes from actively noticing who is being excluded. Whether it's because of gender, race, sexuality, income status, or something else, it's important to look closely at where exclusion is happening and ask yourself why.

Learning at a young age to surround and involve ourselves with those who are different from us is a strong and powerful tool for growth—and a necessary one. The pursuit of equality allows us to expand our minds, open our hearts, and just be better people. And it's never too late (or too early) to get started. So let's talk about gender equality!

Hello, my name is

# BILLIE JEAN KING

I was once the best women's
tennis player in the world.

# I WAS #1 for 5 years.

I won 39 of the biggest and best tournaments in the world— they're called Grand Slam events.

And one time, I played against a guy named Bobby Riggs while 90 million people watched.

Most people said I didn't have a chance, but I won...

BY A LOT.

Even though I did all that,
when I wake up in the morning,
I just think of myself as a kid
from Long Beach, California.

I'm a 79-year-old woman now, but I remember being an 11-year-old girl.

A kid with dreams of becoming the #1 tennis player in the world.

My mom and dad supported me and my tennis dreams, even when that was pretty uncommon for a girl.

My dad was a firefighter and a really good athlete.

My mom worked hard and was a great athlete too, but she never talked about it.

I always wondered WHY...

I also wondered about other things...

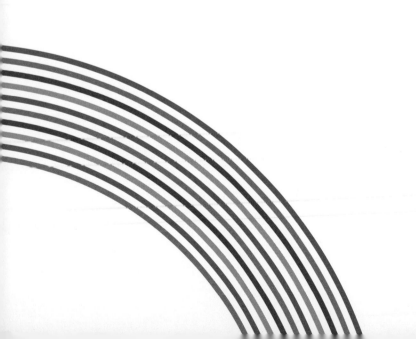

Like why moms stayed home with the kids and the dads went to work.

(That's what it was like when I was a kid back in the 1950s.)

Or why when I went to professional baseball games, no women ever got to play.

(It's still a lot like that today.)

Do you know why?

I didn't know what to call it when
I was a kid. No one ever told me.

But you seem like a smart kid,
so I'll tell you.

# INEQUALITY.

It's a strange word, I know.

It looks like the world "equal" with a bunch of other letters added.

"Inequality" is when
something is not equal.

When something is:

# NOT FAIR,

# NOT JUST,

# NOT GOOD,

# AND NOT RIGHT...

What I noticed when I was a kid was that things weren't equal.

Not for women and men.

Not for girls and boys.

And guess what?

# THINGS ARE BETTER NOW, BUT STILL NOT TRULY EQUAL...

Inequality happens in lots of ways, all the time, all around you.

It happens so much, you might not even notice it.

Don't believe me? ═══════⟹

Did you know that many women make less money than men, even when they do the same job?

# THE
# SAME
# JOB!!

Women often work harder
for the same opportunities.

Women often don't get
the same support.

Women often don't get
the same respect.

And it's even harder for women
of color and women with disabilities.

I wish this weren't true, but it is.

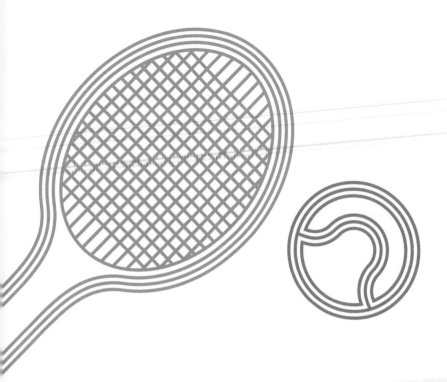

I experienced inequality
in tennis too!

When I won 1 of the biggest tennis
tournaments in the world,
I got paid £750.*

*The symbol £ means "pound sterling," the money
in the UK. And you say it like this: 750 pounds.

But guess how much the man who won the same tournament got?

£2,000!

That's not fair.

**That's not equality.**

I could have just been angry
(which I was), but I also...

DID SOMETH

ING ABOUT IT..

I decided I couldn't work for unfair pay.

And I knew inequality wasn't right.

We needed our own
tournaments where
we were paid fairly.

In 1970, with the support of our friend and promoter, Gladys Heldman,
9 tennis players:

ROSIE CASALS,
PEACHES BARTKOWICZ,
JULIE HELDMAN,
KERRY MELVILLE REID,
ME, BILLIE JEAN KING,
VALERIE ZIEGENFUSS,
KRISTY PIGEON,
NANCY RICHEY,
& JUDY TEGART DALTON,

decided to fight for 3 things:

1. A place to compete.

2. To be appreciated for our accomplishments, not just our looks.

3. To make a living doing what we love.

People told us we couldn't do it.

THEY WERE

# WRONG...

It wasn't easy, but we fought to be paid as much as the men for 1 reason...

We believed in equality.

Equality is when everyone has the same opportunities, rights, and status.

That's the grownup way of saying,

"BE KIND AND BE GOOD."

Even though we fought to help make things more equal, there's still lots more work to do.

You see...

Little boys are still told to be brave,
and grow up to start companies,
and play in the major leagues.

Little girls are still told to be perfect,
and many are told to start families
and raise children when they grow up.

And kids who identify as non-binary
kind of get left in the dark.

This is wrong, because kids are told what they can do or should be based on their gender.

# THAT"S NOT EQUALITY...

# Can you think of examples where equality is missing around you?

Are there any sports which women aren't allowed to play professionally?

Do your teachers say things like, "That's only for the boys."?

Are there any sports that seem to leave girls and non-binary kids out?

How many women can you count in Congress? (More than ever before! But there still aren't as many women as men.)

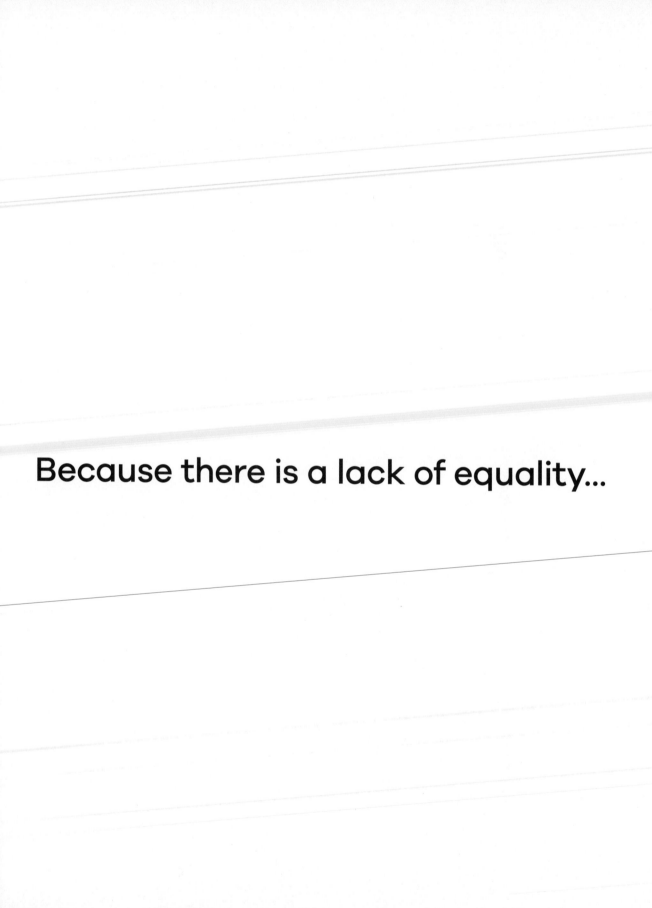

Because there is a lack of equality...

only men have been President of the United States (but we have our first woman Vice President).

more men have been able to start companies than women.

more men are in history books.

men make more money than women.

And I could list 100 more things—1,000 more things—about the inequality between men and everyone else.

But that doesn't mean equality
is impossible to achieve.

That doesn't mean we
should give up. Right?!

Because...

**everyone should feel included.**

**everyone matters.**

**we all have a role to play.**

**equality is worth it.**

You might be thinking to yourself...

*What can I do?*

It turns out you can
actually do a lot.

The first thing you
can do is notice.

# NOTICE

when someone is left out
because of their gender.

# NOTICE

when someone says,
"That's not for you."

# NOTICE

when there isn't equality.

Pay attention and notice, because what you pay attention to grows and becomes more important. And then...

# DO SOMETHI

You can do something about inequality whether you're a boy, or a girl, or are non-binary—no matter how you identify.

Everyone can share their power, voice, and support.

We can all be courageous and choose to show up and speak up.

# GROWNUPS, EMPOWER KIDS TO DREAM BIG AND SEEK EQUALITY.

Every kid deserves
excitement, investment,
and encouragement!

Because we...

BELIEVE IN
EQUALITY...

# Outro
## for grownups

**I**nequality is uncomfortable to talk about, but I can think of no conversation more important to start when kids are young. Our kids today have the power and capability to build a world that looks different—more accepting, more diverse, and more beautiful.

Encourage the kid in your life to believe there is nothing they can't do, and nothing they "should" be. They were born to be them, with all their passions, gifts, and loves, and when they bravely step into that, no matter their gender, they are actively creating a more equal world. And that's amazing!

If you can, support your kids in whatever it is they want to pursue. Gender stereotypes are just that—stereotypes. Allowing your kids to be who they are is equality in action.

Keep the conversation going around equality, and know you are raising the next generation of leaders, problem-solvers, innovators, and influencers. I can't wait to see what they come up with.

Let's go for it!

# About The Author

Billie Jean King (she/her) is a lifelong champion of equality. She uses her platform as one of the greatest and most recognized tennis players in the world to fight for equal rights and opportunities for all. From her roots in Long Beach, California, to leading the journey for equal prize money at the world's 4 Grand Slam tennis tournaments, to opening new doors for women in sports, King has committed her life to showing up, speaking up, and making a difference in the lives of others.

She is the first female athlete to receive the Presidential Medal of Freedom. King is part of the ownership group of the Los Angeles Dodgers baseball team, and Angel City FC soccer team. She founded the Women's Tennis Association, the Women's Sports Foundation, and the Billie Jean King Leadership Initiative Foundation.

King wrote this book to empower the next generation and their grownups.